The
Fifth
Act
Players

by
Susan Blackaby

photographed by
Ken Karp

MODERN CURRICULUM PRESS

Pearson Learning Group

The fifth graders at King School formed a drama club that met every Tuesday in Mr. Chin's classroom. They elected Rita Rios as club president and Barry Stanton as treasurer, and Sara Bell volunteered to be the recorder. They named themselves the Fifth Act Players, which Sara wrote on a notebook in large, block letters.

"Now what?" asked Barry.

"We act!" Rita replied.

In the fall, the Fifth Act Players put on a Frog and Toad puppet show for the little kids in the housing project. Otherwise, they were off to a slow start.

"We need ideas," said Rita. "Does anyone have any suggestions?"

It was cold, rainy day. Jojo traced and retraced pictures on a steamy window pane. Barry was trying to balance a pencil on his finger, while Liza braided Sara's hair.

Mr. Chin was grading papers at his desk. "You should do a play," he said.

"Good idea," said Kenny. "I'll be Romeo."

He knelt down and clasped his hands together. "Hey, Juliet! Come to the window!"

"I'm Juliet's daddy," said Jojo. "Yo, Romeo! You don't live in this project! You go home and I mean right now. Do you read me, man?"

"Sorry, Jul," said Kenny. "I've gotta go."

Liza folded her arms, tossed her head, and stuck her nose in the air. "Ask me not whether I care, for you will find I careth not," she said.

"That isn't exactly what I had in mind," said Mr. Chin, laughing. "I think you guys could create a quality play. You just have to put some effort into it."

"Wow!" said Barry. "You mean write our own play? That'd be awesome! Sara, take this down: Act one, scene one; the setting is a classroom, and the characters are Rita, Sara, Jojo, Kenny, Liza, Barry."

"Boy," said Liza, "how original can you get?"

"Now wait," said Mr. Chin. "It's a start."

"He's right," said Rita. "My dad's a writer, and he says you should write about what you know. We are experts when it comes to us."

"Let's do it then," said Jojo.

Everyone got busy. Rita's dad helped them work on the script, while Liza made sketches of the costumes and got the props. Jojo designed the sets, and he and Kenny painted the scenery.

Work on the play was humming along quite well. Then Ms. Silver and one of her students showed up to watch as Kenny and Sara rehearsed.

Ms. Silver was advisor to the Citizenship Club. "We have a proposal for you," she said. "Our club is working with the city council."

"We're trying to earn money for a city clean-up," said Dolly, "and are organizing a Sidewalk Sweep. We want to paint over the graffiti at the project on Hunter Avenue, and we think maybe you could put on your play as a council fundraiser."

"You mean for people?" asked Rita. "On a real stage?"

"Well, sure," said Dolly. "You could come to the city council meeting with us so we can present the idea together. We've already applied for the theater space, and maybe we can get some matching funds from the city."

"Wow!" said Kenny. He gave Dolly and Liza a high five. "This is great!"

"Let me get this straight," said Rita. "You mean put on our play on a real stage, for people in real theater seats?"

Jojo put a hand on Rita's shoulder, then snapped his fingers in front of her nose. "Rita! Rita! Pay attention!"

"Okay, so what do we need to do?" asked Sara.

"Well, isn't it obvious?" asked Barry. "We have to finish the play, and pull together about twenty bazillion details, that's all."

"I mean besides that," said Sara.

"Besides that, nothing," said Dolly. "We can help with publicity. And since we already applied for the theater space, you don't have that to worry about either."

"What do you say, guys?" asked Liza.

Everyone looked at each other and then nodded, even Rita.

"Okay, then," said Kenny. "You're on!"

"You mean *you're* on," said Dolly, laughing.

Dolly and Ms. Silver left. Mr. Chin leaned against a desk.

"You know," he said, "this is a terrific opportunity for you guys. A play is incomplete without an audience."

"A play is incomplete without a last act," said Sara.

"Sharpen your pencil, girl," said Jojo, rubbing his hands together. "We have a play to finish!"

On opening night, Jojo was putting the last touches on the scenery as Liza and Kenny were hunting for the baseball bat prop. Rita was going over lines with Barry one more time, and Sara was reviewing a checklist to make sure they hadn't forgotten anything.

"It looks like a big crowd," said Sara. "We'll have money for painting that project soon."

"And I am just the guy to do it," said Jojo, waving a paintbrush.

Dolly came backstage. "I just wanted to tell you all to shake a leg," she said.

"She means 'break a leg,'" said Kenny. "That's theater talk for 'good luck.'"

"No, I mean shake a leg," said Dolly. "That's mom talk for 'get moving,' because it's almost time."

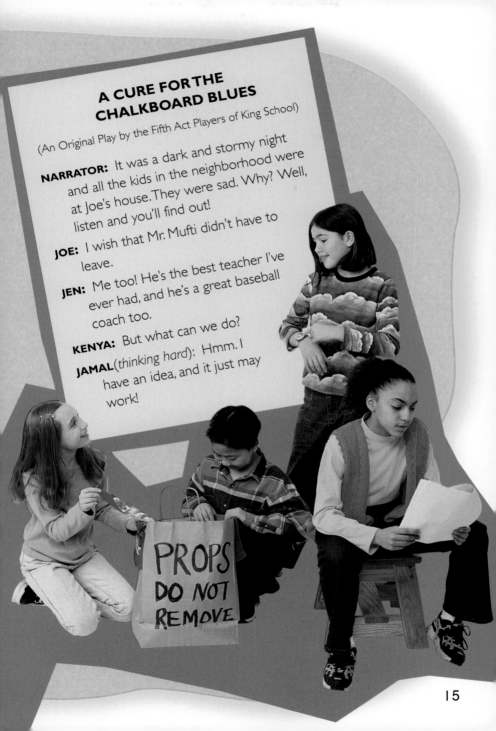

A CURE FOR THE CHALKBOARD BLUES

(An Original Play by the Fifth Act Players of King School)

NARRATOR: It was a dark and stormy night and all the kids in the neighborhood were at Joe's house. They were sad. Why? Well, listen and you'll find out!

JOE: I wish that Mr. Mufti didn't have to leave.

JEN: Me too! He's the best teacher I've ever had, and he's a great baseball coach too.

KENYA: But what can we do?

JAMAL *(thinking hard):* Hmm. I have an idea, and it just may work!

PROPS DO NOT REMOVE

15

Dolly popped through the curtain.

"Good evening and welcome to *A Cure for the Chalkboard Blues,* an original play by the Fifth Act Players of King School."

Dolly finished her introduction and came back through the curtain.

"We are all set," said Rita. "Jojo and Liza, take your places, and everyone else clear the stage."

Kenny waved to Mr. Chin, then threw the switch to dim the lights.

"This is it!" said Dolly. "You're the best! Oh, and guys? Break a leg!"